# Freddy the Frog

Story by Janie Spaht Gill, Ph.D.
Illustrations by Bob Reese

🔴 Dominie Press, Inc.

Freddy the frog
jumped onto a log.

3

The log sank,
so he jumped onto a bank.

# The bank was steep,

so he jumped into a jeep.

# The jeep went fast,

so he jumped into the grass.

The grass was tall,
so he jumped onto a wall.

The wall was big,
so he jumped onto a twig.

# The twig was bent,
# so he jumped into a tent.

The tent was round,

so he jumped onto a clown.

The clown bowed,
so he jumped into the crowd.

19

# The crowd ran away,

and Freddy decided to stay.

# Freddy the Frog

- Retell the story of *Freddy the Frog* using drama. Each child could draw a frog on a sheet of construction paper, color it green, cut it out, and then glue it to a Popsicle stick. The class could practice story sequencing by hopping to the various places and events depicted in the story.

- Use this opportunity to explain the stages in the life of a frog: egg, tadpole, and adult frog. You could also talk about the metamorphosis of a caterpillar into a butterfly: egg, larva, pupa, and adult butterfly.

- Recreate the sequence of the story by making a "skinny strip." This is a strip of adding machine paper about three feet long. The children divide it into as many sections as there are events in the book, plus one. (In this case, there are ten events.) The first section is for the title, the author, and a child's name listed as the illustrator. Have the children draw a picture in each section, retelling the sequence of the story.

- Make a story web. Start by putting the word *frog* in the center of a circle. Then draw lines running out from the circle with events written on them. The overall appearance is much like that of the sun with its light radiating in all directions.

## *About the Author*

*Dr. Janie Spaht Gill brings twenty-five years of teaching experience to her books for young children. During her career thus far, she has taught at every grade level, from kindergarten through college. Gill has a Ph.D. in reading education, with a minor in creative writing. She is currently residing in Lafayette, Louisiana with her husband, Richard. Her fresh, humorous topics are inspired by the things her students say in the classroom. Gill was voted the 1999-2000 Louisiana Elementary Teacher of the Year for her outstanding work in primary education.*

Publisher: Raymond Yuen
Editorial Consultant: Adria F. Klein
Editor: Bob Rowland
Designer: Natalie Chupil
Illustrator: Bob Reese

Published by:

## ℗ Dominie Press, Inc.

1949 Kellogg Avenue
Carlsbad, California 92008 USA

www.dominie.com
(800) 232-4570

Softcover Edition ISBN 0-7685-2153-X
Library Bound Edition ISBN 0-7685-2461-X


Printed in Singapore by PH Productions Pte Ltd
1 2 3 4 5 6  PH  05 04 03

| Dominie Level | Guided Reading | DeFord Assessment |
|---------------|----------------|-------------------|
| 10            | F              | 5                 |